T0199180

The Colorful Counting book

2 1 4 10 6 3 5 7 9 8

Tracy Coulson

Illustrated by Shannen Marie Paradero

To order additional copies of this book, contact:
Xlibris
1-888-795-4274
www.Xlibris.com
Orders@Xlibris.com

ISBN: Softcover   978-1-7960-9036-9
           EBook   978-1-7960-9035-2

Print information available on the last page

Rev. date: 02/25/2020

1

Red Fire Truck

1 Red firetruck

2

Yellow Ducks

2 Yellow ducks

3

Three Blue Ribbons

3 Blue Ribbons

4

Four Purple Flowers

4 Purple flowers

5

Five White Snowflakes

5 white snowflakes

Six Green Baby Turtles

6 Green baby Turtles

7

7 Black kittens

8

Eight Golden Fish

8 Gold fish

9

Nine Brown Footballs

9 Brown footballs

10

Ten Orange Pumpkins

Orange pumkins

2 1 4 10 6 5 3 8 7 9

The End

Printed in the United States
By Bookmasters